BURDENS & BLESSINGS

HOWARD MILLER

BURDENS & BLESSINGS

A LIGHTER-HEARTED APPROACH FOR MIDDLE-AGED FOLKS DEALING WITH AGING PARENTS

HOWARD MILLER

Copyright © 2024 by Howard Miller

All rights reserved. No part of this publication may be reproduced, distributed, or transmitted in any form or by any means, or stored in a database or retrieval system, without the prior written permission of the copyright holder, except by a reviewer who may quote brief passages in a review.

It'll work out.
And if it doesn't work out,
it worked out.

*Said by George Miller to my brother Andy
in early July 2021, a few weeks before
my dad passed at 99 years old.*

To Lila and George Miller.

Words alone don't express what I want to say.

I love and miss you both.

Contents

BOOK ACKNOWLEDGMENTS	11
FOREWORD	13
OPENING	15
INTRODUCTION	17
THE CHANGE IS GRADUAL	21
WHO'S GOING TO FOLD IT?	23
JOKES AND CONTEMPLATIONS ABOUT DEATH	29
GETTING OLDER	33
HEARING LOSS	35
SCAMMERS	37
TREATING YOUR PARENTS LIKE CHILDREN	41
LIGHT BULBS, AND TVS, AND BATHS, OH MY!	45
SORRY, I HAVE TO TAKE THIS	48
PLAYING MARRIAGE COUNSELOR	51
GETTING TO KNOW THE DOCTORS	53
THE FINANCIAL REALITIES	57
STUMBLES AND FALLS	62
MANAGING THE AIDES	66
FUNERAL ARRANGEMENTS	71
THE PANDEMIC	75
SIBLING RIVALRY	79
DEMENTIA AND STUBBORNNESS	83
HOSPICE	85
GOD FORBID AND GOD WILLING	88
I SAW MY MOM DIE	89
EPILOGUE	95
WHAT I LEARNED ALONG THE WAY	99
THINGS I'M GRATEFUL FOR DURING THIS TIME	100
ABOUT THE AUTHOR	103

Book Acknowledgments

Thanks to Jay Kushner, Richard Cunningham, Delcy Ziac Fox, Eric Keith, and Beth Miller who helped me move my grief forward. Thanks to Delcy for editorial assistance. Thanks to my brother Andy who shared this journey, and to my nieces Savannah and Jessie who will move it forward.

Foreword

The number one reason I'm writing this book is for my healing. To keep me a bit more grounded in my journey of grief and loss. If nothing else results, it will be cathartic for me.

But I'd also like to share my experience in watching two people, my parents, age without any major illness. I got to experience first-hand what all of us will experience if we are fortunate enough to live into our 80s, 90s, and beyond.

It's a part of life we intellectually understand. It's different when you see two people who you have known your entire life, who raised you, who loved you and drove you crazy, go through it. It hits home. It happened to them, so it will happen to me.

Anyone 40 or over might be dealing with parents getting older. My trainer is starting to experience it with his dad (my trainer's dad is about my age, LOL). My family seems to have gotten older later in years, but what happened to my folks in their late 80s continuing into their 90s, can happen to anyone 60 and over, especially those who have not kept themselves in good shape or unfortunately have an illness.

The people I have talked to whose parents have already left this world still want to talk about their experiences, even if it was five-to-ten years ago.

The people I have talked to who are just beginning or who are in the middle of this journey also find comfort in the fact that they aren't alone.

I watched an interview where country singer Tanya Tucker said she took a 17-year break from recording albums after her parents died. Their deaths left her untethered and she lost her mojo because the people she trusted most were gone.

Actress Tovah Feldshuh said the death of her mother (who lived to over 100) made her realize that she had lived more of her life than she had in front of her.

I agree with those sentiments. After my mom's death less than a year and a half after my dad, I find myself reaching for something but never being able to get it.

So, this book is to help me understand. It's to be cathartic by sharing some of my experiences and what I wish I had known. Maybe it will help someone else in their journey.

And of course, I'm hoping that this book leads to talks (including a TED talk!), workshops, and perhaps an entrepreneurial adventure that's yet to be envisioned!!

Opening

Circa 2005, my brother mentioned that we were on borrowed time with our parents (Dad was 83 and Mom was 75). Around the same time, I was taken out to lunch by a longtime friend to celebrate my birthday. I mentioned to him that my parents were like a long running TV show—you wondered why it was still on the air, but when it's finally canceled you miss it. (Actually, I don't think I ever had that type of commitment to a show—I mean, "The Facts of Life," seriously?!)

But my parents were another story.

Around 2006, when my eldest niece Savannah was 5 years old, she was with my folks and asked my dad how old he was. He replied "84." My niece looked at him seriously and, with the unfiltered response of a child, said "You're almost dead!" I'm not sure how my dad reacted, but my mom cracked up.

This was 10 years before any shit really hit the fan.

That wouldn't happen for another 15 years.

This book is about my experience during these 15 years.

Introduction

One of my tennis buddies had a dad around the same age as my dad. He was estranged from his dad. As a result, as I was going through my daily worry, he wasn't. I asked him if, when his dad passes, he would have any regrets and he said, "Not really."

Boy was I jealous!! It seemed at this point in my life (from my 50s to early 60s), while I still had a life, it was overshadowed, every day, sometimes several times a day, by something with my parents, whether it was making phone calls on their behalf, ordering items for them, or mediating conversations between the home care agency or insurance companies on something that needed attention. If that wasn't happening, I was planning my next trip to Los Angeles to see them. If a day went by without being in touch with at least one of my parents, it was few and far between.

How did my life come to this? I had spent most of my adult life as an independent (I was told "fiercely independent," by someone) gay man who had many interests and activities that kept me engaged. Whether I intentionally chose it or not, I only had to answer to me.

Now, don't get me wrong, I come from a very close-knit family. While we had our dysfunctionalities like any other family, there was implicit trust between us.

Despite living long distance from my folks, I saw them regularly, at least every six weeks. I was fortunate to have a job where I traveled, so it wasn't unusual to have a trip, let's say from San Francisco to Michigan, where afterward I would go to New York for the weekend. One of the companies I worked for when I worked full time was headquartered in Stamford, Connecticut, which was close to my folks in New York. As I eloquently put it to my mom, I will see you both regularly until the end.

When my brother, who lives in Los Angeles, had his girls, my parents flew to LA more regularly. I would often go down as well, to see them and my nieces.

So, we were close and were able to see each other, despite the distance.

But there's a difference between this type of relationship versus the type when I became responsible for their safety and then later to running more and more of their daily lives.

I cringed when people said I was a good son. I didn't see myself as a good son, I saw myself as a dutiful son. I'm not sure a good son would be envious of someone who had an estranged relationship with their dad, and therefore he didn't have any responsibility to his elderly parent.

I don't think a good son would remember what another one of his friends said when he was asked about his folks. He said, "my parents had the sense to go at a younger age." Part of me wondered what that would have been like.

I considered myself a dutiful son. I did what was right, so I could live my life without looking back with embarrassment or question what I should have done for my parents.

I made my parents one of my highest priorities as I was going through my middle age.

This wasn't a choice, it just was.

My folks in the back of a limo.

The Change is Gradual

About 20 years ago I was talking to an acquaintance at a party. He was in the midst of dealing with his parents. They both had Alzheimer's and lived in a different state. At this point my folks were older, but completely independent. I had to do nothing to help them.

This guy started to yell, and yell at me, saying "who is going to take care of them?" Looking back, this guy was a little arrogant. So, in this understandably stressful time for him, yelling was the easiest outlet for him (and obviously memorable for me)!

At the time, I thought it was inappropriate that he yelled at me, and he didn't know my situation, but looking back at what he had to say, I realize he was correct.

Who is going to take care of them? Who's going to handle their finances? Who is going to handle their day-to-day?

My parents' independence slowly led to dependence, which led to more and more for my brother and me to do and be responsible for their care.

From 2015 until 2023 I created approximately 350 documents relating to something with my parents.

These documents, in no particular order, covered everything from home care agencies in both Los Angeles and Florida, assisted care and board & care options in LA, notes after talking with the doctor about something going on with one of them, cell phone options, hospice notes, applications for handicap placards (both in Florida and California, I never did figure out if one state would accept the other state's placard), info on the Braille institute in Los Angeles, financial information (such as banks and credit cards), references to the condo in Florida and the apartment in LA, invoices for several home care agencies that had to be submitted for reimbursements, and information on assistive devices for the visually impaired to research on trusts and Medicaid, options for medical alert systems, funeral information, the frequently changed documents on where my mom kept her higher value jewelry (which she kept moving!), not to mention various Word documents where I vented about my frustrations with everything that was happening.

They serve as a memory of the burdens and blessings of these eight years.

Who's Going to Fold It?

One year I was down in Los Angeles the week of Thanksgiving, staying at my folks'. It was unusually cool that week. One afternoon my mom was lying down to take a nap and she said she was cold. I found a blanket and I put it over her. She said, "Thank you." Then she sighed and exclaimed, "Now who's going to fold it?"

Consciously or not, my parents turned to humor in all aspects of their lives. A book in our home growing up was called "Laughter is the Best Medicine."

We could be at the movies and if only two people were laughing at a particular line, it was both my parents.

When things got funny, my mom would tend to snort and that made her laugh harder!

My brother and I kept our parents laughing during the last years of their lives. For example, they enjoyed recording a commercial for my brother's friend's cable TV show. They laughed doing it and their ad libs are priceless to me.

My humor stems from my parents (and 1970s situational comedies, but I don't think I would have connected with those comedies if not for my parents).

When my brother got married, I included a note that many would think was quite bizarre. But it was hilarious to my brother and my folks. This note included the inception of my fictional twin brother Harold. For years to come, any of us might sign Harold's name to any birthday or anniversary card.

As my father got into his mid-90s and sometimes referred to Harold I jokingly said to him, "Dad, you better watch it. I could just say to the authorities I don't know what he's talking about!"

When I was a young adult, there was a toy of a small figurine dressed as an astronaut where you could move the arm to say hello. I don't know if I started it or my dad started it, but we would put it in each other's suitcase so that when we got home it would be there for us. We took turns keeping the astronaut until we passed it back to the other person. This went on for several years until the figurine got lost.

My dad's wit and humor were constant. We have a video where my brother sarcastically asks my dad, "you fought in the Civil War?" Dad quickly said "no, the Revolutionary." He was in his late 90s when this video was made.

When Dad was in the rehab center and in a lot of pain, he got frustrated when my mom answered her phone while he was talking to her. He turned to me and said, "it'll be my funeral, her phone will ring and she'll answer it!!"

When I tried to get him to use a walker or cane (before he broke his hip) and he would give a non-committal answer, I challenged him by asking him how he would feel if I, or Andy, said to him we were going to take all our money, go to Vegas and bet it on red or black. Wouldn't he try and reason with us? He said: no, we are adults. And I said: so, you'd say nothing. His response: no, I'd ask which color you'd bet on.

My dad got a pacemaker when he was 95. He learned how to transmit the results to his doctor before every appointment by reading the manual and by trial and error. Pretty impressive that he was using the internet and modern technology to do that. During one Zoom meeting with the doctor when he was 97 and I was with him in person, he asked the doctor how long the battery in the pacemaker will last. The doctor said another 8 years. My dad's response: what do we do after that?!

My mom had some clams and I told her to give one to Dad. She picked it up and proceeded to eat it herself.

One time, I needed to tell my mom that Andy had Covid. He was fine, but she needed to know. I said to her, *listen I have something to tell you.* Her immediate response was, *what is it?*

Savannah's (who was a teenager at the time) *pregnant?!* That sort of made the actual news not as bad!

Another time I was driving from San Francisco to Los Angeles. This was in 2016, shortly after my dad broke his hip and was in the rehab facility. After my 6-to-7 hours' drive, I stopped at my mom's to drop off my stuff before I went to see my dad. Mom was at their place as she wasn't feeling great and stayed home that day. As soon as I walked in, the first thing she said was, *Howard those shorts are ugly.* I replied, *I thought you couldn't see.* She retorted, *oh Howard, one doesn't have to see to know how hideous they are!"*

Everything wasn't always funny, especially for my mom as her pain increased. But she was funny whether she realized it or not.

When I said to her out of concern that I had never seen her in so much pain as she was right then, her response was, *you didn't see me when I gave birth to you!*

The last time I took her to the doctor, which was a couple of months before she passed, we left the doctor and she told me she was feeling depressed. I replied by saying it made sense that she felt depressed, look at all the shit that happened since Dad passed. She looked at me earnestly and said, *if I could only shit.*

To her that remark wasn't funny, and I get that. But the fact that I laughed at that moment, made her laugh at that moment, so for that moment, she was filled with laughter.

What a gift that is for me, what a gift I gave her in that moment, and what a gift they both gave to us about the benefits of humor.

Humor has always helped me through pain, times of grief and times of self-doubt, insecurity, and loneliness. For me humor is a powerful tool that represents hope and moving forward and living life.

I did conscious breathing or "rebirthing" as it was once called, a couple of times in my 30s and 40s. I remember the first time I did it I was so nervous. I was in a room with over 100 people and as soon as we started some people were wailing, screaming, and crying. It freaked me out. Luckily, I was in the group of first timers, so I was guided along. As I relaxed, the Chuckles the Clown funeral scene from "The Mary Tyler Moore Show" came into my memory. I started to laugh hysterically. Then I started to sob. Then I started to laugh.

I repeated this pattern of laughter and sobbing in a much smaller group (about 20 people) at a later time, without Chuckles the Clown. But I would burst into hysterical laughter and then in the middle of the laughter would start to sob uncontrollably which would then turn into hysterical laughter. Apparently, this affected everyone in the room who also started laughing and sobbing!

I have found my humor to guide me through grief.

When my dad died, I was making arrangements for his body to be shipped from Los Angeles to New York. The helpful woman at the funeral home was giving me the logistics, saying he was on a flight that transferred in Denver and then landed in New York.

My response: Does he get a meal?!

Her response: Nobody ever asked me that!!

I know my dad would have loved that moment!

This gift has been passed down. When my brother Andy, niece Jessie, and I were going to visit my parents' graves, we had trouble finding them. We were in the correct location but couldn't find the exact spot. My brother took off to look and Jessie (who did eventually find where they were buried) kept looking where we were. My niece looked at me as we were searching and said "should we call her?!"

I'm sure my parents laughed and smiled in that moment.

As I'm writing this, I'm laughing and tearing up at the same time. And Mom and Dad are right here with me doing the same.

Ultimately, the gift of humor is helping me heal.

Would you vote for this man?!

Jokes and Contemplations about Death

My father would always say that getting older is better than the alternative.

For several years I played an annual game that a friend's brother coordinated. Basically, by midnight December 31 you must pick 10 famous people who you thought would die the following year. It was all based on 120 points (120 representing 120 years), so the younger the person was, the more points you would get. The person with the most points at the end of the year got the cash prize (everyone donated $10 and there were anywhere between 15 to 30 people involved in this morbid, fun contest).

And it was morbid! I tried to find famous people who no one else would pick. So, I found myself getting excited when Mary Fickett, one of the original cast members of *All My Children* died. I almost lost my professional cool when I was in a class and got a text that Andy Williams had died. I was so excited because I knew I was the only one who had picked him, and I had been monitoring his health. I started smiling and the person sitting next to me asked what was going on. I just grinned and said "Andy Williams just died!"

So many people feigned horror at this game, yet their fascination never wavered. For the five years I played this game (and won once), people would text me after someone famous died and ask if I had picked them.

Personally, I loved this game, not just because others would be shocked by it, but I know that since death will have the last laugh on all of us, we might as well have fun with it!

My dad was in his late 80s to early 90s while all of this was going on, and his reaction was one of a parent: he just shrugged his shoulders as if to say *I love my child, I did my best, I take no responsibility for this.*

The only comment he made to me was, "Don't put my name down on your list."

My response was don't worry, you're not famous and you're too old, I won't get enough points!

I don't believe this lighthearted joking lessened the seriousness or stress of the last several years, but I do know that through it all we did have levity. Through the pain and uncertainty, we found humor at various times, even for just a moment. Whether it was something one of us said, or listening to a Don Rickles stand-up routine, or watching a familiar movie like *What's Up, Doc?*, those moments brought us together and made us feel more human.

2014, Mom 84, Dad 92!

Getting Older

It takes a little more to do a little less. After 40, we start to feel it in a variety of physical and emotional ways. For example, for me, driving on the highway at night has increased my anxiety as I've aged.

But I know I've only touched the surface of what that statement "it takes a little more to do a little less" means. Imagine what this will be like in your 80s and 90s?

Most people reading this might not grasp the meaning of this statement because they haven't experienced it significantly.

Prior to my parents needing to rely on others (when they were both in their 80s), my parents used to joke with me and said things like "how does it feel hanging around with old people?!"

Reflecting on that, they weren't old at the time they said this. They were older, and probably older than how long a lot of people live, but they weren't that old. Someone that old wouldn't say something like that.

When my dad got into his 90s, especially after he broke his hip, and my mom got into her later 80s, this kind of talk stopped.

All of us take the everyday for granted. We experience subtle changes—with our bodies and with our memory. They don't happen all at once. But how we think we will be when we are older, we won't really know until we are older.

It's like when you know you are going to go through a tough time or situation and then you actually go through it. The pre thought about it is not the experience.

For any of us to think of how we will be is incomprehensible. After all, the world will be very different in 20- or 30-years' time.

But losing one's ability to do common tasks is one thing to think about, another to experience.

My folks were lucky. They were both functional until the end. They could dress themselves and my mom could shower on her own.

But I could do 5-10 activities in the time it took them to do one activity!

We all need to feel significant in our lives. Many people get that from their job. For others it's power, travel, or money.

When you get to a certain age, you still need significance, but it's different.

I often asked one of my parents what they did that morning, and the response was "I had breakfast."

They were serious. That's what they did.

For them, it was enough.

One might be judgmental about this or find it depressing, but it's kind of cool when you think about it. They get the same satisfaction from doing something that we might think mundane as we get when we do something that could be much more complex, stressful, and time consuming.

Neither is better, it seems to me it's what we need at different times in our lives.

Hearing Loss

When I was in my early 50s, I often thought that my tennis opponents were saying 40, when they were actually saying 30. I realized that my hearing had diminished to where I couldn't distinguish between those two words. I figured out what they said based on the side they were serving from. Since then, I have noticed others question the score and I realized they were going through the same thing I had but hadn't realized it was their hearing that was the problem, not that an incorrect score was called!

That was when I was in my 50s. At the time, my folks were in their 80s and 90s and they refused to get hearing aids. They joked about the loss of hearing. Truthfully much of it was pretty funny.

My mom to my dad: I heard Levine (her doctor) came by yesterday.

Dad: You're in pain?

Me to Dad: A friend of mine is turning 65.

Dad: What? He died?

Me to Dad: Do you know you still have phone books from Rockland County?

Dad: I have to go to the bathroom.

Me: She won't cook your dinner?

Dad: I'll have cookies.

Dad: You didn't ask if I had a key.

Mom: You need to pee?

Me: She called me while I was on break.

Dad: How is Blake?

Mom to Dad: Is Howard here?
        Dad: I'm fine how are you?
      Andy: So, when will you use the hearing aid I got you?
        Dad: What did you say? (I'm not sure if this was an intentional response from Dad!)

You can't make this stuff up. These all came from not hearing what the other person said.

But there is the reality of a very loud TV.

When I came over to my parents' place, the two things I did almost immediately was to lower the heat and to lower the volume on the TV.

I do believe their lives would have been enhanced if they had gotten hearing aids. My brother pushed my dad to get them, but to no avail. It wasn't until Dad passed, that my brother thought our dad may not have wanted them so he could avoid hearing our mom! I support that conclusion.

While the purpose of hearing aids is to enhance our hearing, it's a personal decision that each person has to make. I hope I am more open to getting a hearing aid when I need it or at least from 10 years from when I need it.

Scammers

There are so many scammers out there. Via email, via text, via the phone. What sad and pathetic people these scammers are that they are reduced to trying to rip off others.

Obviously, it works otherwise they wouldn't keep doing it.

While we were concerned about either of my parents getting scammed, especially Mom after Dad passed, we did have a piece of history that everyone remembered that was a cautionary tale.

My grandmother, my mom's mother, was a victim of elder fraud. While my grandma was walking on the street, another older showed my grandmother what she "found," which was a lot of money.

How this woman communicated with my grandma is puzzling since my grandmother was part of the deaf community.

How she let my grandma take her up to her apartment is very perplexing.

Then they went to the bank, and against the bank teller's wishes, my grandmother withdrew a lot of money.

My mom was called, my grandmother was embarrassed.

I don't know how much money was stolen.

I know I wished I had randomly dropped by that day. I would have punched that lady from one side of the street to the other.

I know my mom never forgot that incident.

So I had something to bring up to her to remind her to be careful.

Most of us ignore calls from numbers we don't recognize. I get texts almost daily with a hello that I ignore.

When you can't see, you answer the phone.

There were times my mom agreed to send money to a charity. But she said they needed to mail her something. Of course they didn't.

One time when I was there, she got one of those calls. I took the phone and told the person at the other end never to call again.

If everything does happen for a reason, then my grandma being scammed happened so that being careful hit home for all of us, especially Mom.

Relaxing in Andy's backyard during the pandemic.

Treating your Parents like Children

My dad's hygiene started to decline, especially after he broke his hip. From what I understand, good personal hygiene can be challenging as you get older, for a variety of reasons, including lack of mobility and lack of energy.

I would get on my dad about this from time to time, but it became more serious after the VA aide was no longer able to come to the house to shower my dad. He tried to get another aide, but it could be weeks before one was secured. I got Dad to agree to let Mom's aide who came every day to help Dad shower. This was the aide from my mom's agency where we paid extra for her to look after my dad also. But my dad just thought she was there for Mom, he didn't need the help. He preferred to shower in the morning, but I tried to convince Dad, or pleaded, to take the shower in the afternoon when mom's aide was there.

So he told me that he did take a shower one day when the aide came.

When I mentioned it to my mom the next day, she said he didn't take a shower.

I then talked to my dad and the conversation went something like this:

>Me: Didn't you tell me you took a shower with the aide yesterday?
>
>Dad: Yes.
>
>Me: But you didn't take a shower.
>
>Dad: No.
>
>Me: So, you lied?
>
>Dad: Yes!

Fortunately, I didn't get upset—I chuckled a bit (I think I would've been upset if he just didn't straight out and calmly say that he lied).

Really, can you blame him?

When I was younger, I would get lectured at by him or my mother and I sometimes would say something to shut them up.

Now he's doing it to me. The roles are reversed. When did this happen?!

My mom once told one of her aides not to come that day because it was too windy out. I checked the weather in Los Angeles and it wasn't true, my mom thought this because she was on the 4th floor and a tree near her window sways in the wind. She got angry at me because I reversed her decision. I had called the aide and told her to go to Mom's, and moving forward, if something like this happened again to contact me so we could determine what should be done.

Although it happens gradually, you find you become the parents of your parents. As a result, they are always under a microscope, which really isn't fair. Imagine if someone was observing everything you did in your home and evaluating each mundane activity that you do.

I remember many years ago, my brother was visiting me, and we had gone shopping and bought a few bottles of the same beverage. My habit is to put one in the refrigerator, and the others on a shelf. His habit is to put them all in the refrigerator. We had a good laugh as he put the second bottle in the refrigerator, and I took it out and put it on a shelf and then he put the third bottle in the refrigerator, and I took it out and put it on a shelf.

Imagine if his habit or mine were evaluated. It's just something that we do, it doesn't need to be examined.

I found myself looking at each thing my parents did and evaluating if it was safe for them to do it. They were living under a microscope. My brother and I would have discussions on how they walked, things they remembered (or didn't remember), their hygiene, how they ate their food, how they put on their clothes, how they tied their shoes, and so on.

I'm guessing we were more critical of them as older adults then they were of us when we were children.

Is it necessary? Yes, at times.

Is it stressful? Always.

What I gradually learned is to pick what was essential to bring up to them. Some things I observed, I may not mention. If I felt they were in danger, I would say something. If either of them mentioned something that was getting difficult for them to do, I might take that opportunity to bring something else up. It rarely was acted upon, but occasionally it was.

So, I tried to accept that most of the things that were brought up would just be ignored.

Emphasize the word "tried."

While I don't have children of my own, I know this is like letting kids fail so they could grow.

Bringing up what was essential allows them to still have their voice. In the book "Being Mortal," by Atul Gawande, he mentioned that, sometimes as people get older, all they have are their choices to make, and they want to make them, whether they are good decisions or not.

When my dad was 94, he broke his hip in June in Los Angeles. In November, both my parents wanted to go to Florida after Thanksgiving.

I thought this was INSANE.

But after I read Gawande's book, I stopped arguing with them. I accepted their decision, put aside whether or not I felt it was a good decision, and made the arrangements (and traveled with them).

This significantly decreased my stress and I actually enjoyed my mom's perplexity about my sudden reversal of not fighting them.

And that truth was, it was a good decision for them. They got to enjoy Florida and did for a few years after that as well.

My parents had the right to stand up for themselves. When they were staying at my brother's at the height of the pandemic, my brother walked in to talk with them and my mom told him they still had a right to their privacy, please don't just walk in.

My mom also didn't like when the aides who helped them would sit at the table when they were eating. She felt it was an invasion of her privacy (unless she invited them to sit with her).

This didn't seem like a big deal to me, but pondering this, I can see where sitting and talking while eating would be a semblance of the familiar for my folks. It was a symbol of normalcy and was of great importance for them to do as long as they could. I'm glad my mom stood up for them.

In my last conversation with her, before she went unresponsive, when she was in the ambulance, she said to the ambulance driver, *can I have some privacy, please?!*

Parents will need help and direction. But they also need to be allowed to express and demand things that are important to them.

Light Bulbs, and TVs, and Baths, Oh My!

When my dad was in his 80s, he told me he noticed that something that took a few minutes in the past, now could take half the morning.

Again, things we take for granted become more monumental as you age.

This was especially true for them when changing light bulbs, figuring out cell phones, turning on the television, and bathing.

It seemed to me my parents were constantly needing light bulbs changed. Is this because they were home more? Mercifully my dad stopped changing bulbs where it required that he get on a ladder. But he would try to change other ones, which could take an extremely long time due to his limited eyesight.

A bigger issue for them was using their cell phones. Whether it was the technology, or their limited eyesight, there was a 50/50 chance they wouldn't answer their phone. At least they could call back after they missed the call, which was often the case.

They had Samsung Galaxy phones. My mom learned to use Google (Hey Google) because she couldn't see the Contacts in the phone.

I spent many hours researching phones for seniors with poor eyesight, seniors with beginning stages of dementia, and phones that could handle both, but I didn't find any phone that would make it easier for them and give them everything they wanted. A couple of phones I researched were the Jitterbug and RAZ memory cell phones.

After my dad died, I switched Mom to an iPhone—she thought it was harder to use, but she got along better with Siri than with Hey Google!

I was in the habit, once my parents were both in their 80s, that if I called both their cell phones and neither of them answered, I would say to myself, "ok, that's it, they're dead."

This isn't what I really believed at the time, but just how I reacted. (It was the same when either of them was napping and I had to get closer to them to make sure they were breathing!)

But as they got older, and they didn't answer, and didn't call back pretty quickly, I would get a little nervous. For the sake of preserving my sanity, I learned how not to get that nervous—if something happened, I would find out about it eventually, so there's no sense worrying about it.

Well, at least I tried that attitude. It worked sometimes.

When my mom went to make a phone call to a business (usually a doctor or physical therapist) and they didn't have a way to speak an option (1, 2, or 3) and instead had to press a selection, my mom couldn't do it. She couldn't see the phone to do this.

Turning on the television was the activity that my parents did most. One false move and they couldn't watch television. If the wrong remote were used, or the television/cable input were accidentally changed, my dad figured the television was broken. Sometimes an aide could figure it out, and sometimes my dad called the cable company.

After my dad's passing, my mom could manage the television only sometimes. It was more daunting for her because of her lack of eyesight. She would get anxious when she heard the television but couldn't see anything. I needed to explain to her that she was listening to music through Alexa and the television wasn't on.

One day my mom went to take a bath. When she wanted to leave the tub, she didn't have the muscle strength to get out. She called to my dad. He couldn't get her out. They called Sam, my brother's friend who lived in their complex. He came over to help her out (she covered herself to keep her modesty and decorum).

You would think this incident would have made my folks realize Mom shouldn't take a bath unless an aide was there. But no, they thought it was hilarious this happened!

Over time, my mom did realize she should only take a bath when the aide was there. I'm not sure if that's because Sam moved away or if that was coincidence.

I said to my dad, you can't do this, you can't expect Sam to drop everything to go over to you. My dad's response was "why, he doesn't mind!" Oy vey.

I was concerned about my dad taking a shower on his own when I took them back to Florida. He didn't argue about my concern, instead when he went to shower he said, *Howard come see your father naked!*

So I figured he was okay to shower on his own.

This was before he broke his hip. After that he needed assistance.

All these things that someone in their 50s or 60s takes for granted, and my parents had taken for granted for so long, became their day's activities as they became more dependent on others to help them.

I wonder what technologies our generation will find complex that the younger folks will be venting about to their peers.

Sorry, I Have to Take This

As my parents became less independent and I took on more and more of the responsibilities, it was a struggle to balance my life with everything that needed to be done, but I knew that it was important to do. Financially, socially, and for my well-being.

But interruptions became more frequent. There was many a tennis game where I had to keep my phone on (which I loath to do) because I was expecting a call from one of their doctors or was waiting for an update from an appointment they were on.

When playing bridge, you weren't allowed to keep your phone on, but I kept it on vibrate for the very same reasons.

A friend reminded me that a month or two before my mom passed, I was on the phone with my mom about 10 times each day, either talking to her, her aides, her doctors, or making appointments. This was while I was on vacation.

People were understanding, or I didn't really give the option not to be.

I stopped shutting my phone off at night, just in case.

I'm not saying it was non-stop, but it was continual.

It was waiting for the other shoe to drop. And it doesn't drop fast. It's slow and gradual but these occurrences get more frequent and the time in between shorter and shorter.

Before either of my folks died, but after my dad broke his hip and was out of rehab, I was teaching an in-person class. At the beginning of the class, I happened to glance at my phone and saw my brother had called. I then noticed my mom had called, too.

My pulse starting racing.

At the first moment I could, I checked their messages. Within a microsecond, I saw there was nothing wrong and it was just coincidence that they both had called.

My brother often wondered why I felt guarded or on edge when I answered his calls. I told him it was because I was expecting bad news.

I made a pact with my mom that I would let her know when I was teaching and she shouldn't call me those days, I would call her (which I did, at lunch, on breaks, or the end of the day).

Reflecting back, this was probably the biggest burden to endure—the constant reminder of what I had no control over, what I couldn't plan, and that it was only going to get more time consuming.

I don't miss this. It zapped my energy and stressed me out.

And it could have been a lot worse.

We all know (at least I hope we do) that self-care is vital, and I still have a lot of that.

Upon reflection, I wish I had been more forgiving of myself for everything going on. When you are in grief, a lot of the books state to be gentle with yourself. I believe this applies to when you are taking responsibility for your parents as well.

I could have used that reminder.

Honeymoon, 1957.

Playing Marriage Counselor

In "The Lion in Winter," Katherine Hepburn as Eleanor of Aquitaine, famously says "What family doesn't have its ups and downs?"

I learned, perhaps too many times, don't get involved in other people's relationships.

This especially applies to Mom and Dad.

Their relationship is their relationship.

But as they got older, less independent, and were constantly around each other, sometimes an intervention was necessary.

Both, at different times, lashed out at the other, to the extent where I had to reprimand them. My saving moment was one time my dad said to me after one reprimand, "You handled that well!"

On the flip side there is a memory I'll always cherish.

About a week after my dad broke his hip and had his surgery, he was in a rehab facility. I was down in Los Angeles; it was the beginning of his rehab stint so it was all very new. As my mom and I were leaving for the day, my dad grabbed my mom and started to cry, saying he didn't think he could do this, meaning the recovery.

I left the room to give them privacy, but of course I listened in.

My mom was beautifully empathetic in that moment. She held his hand, let him cry, didn't argue with him, and mostly listened to him.

It was one of those rare moments we all have had with special people in our lives.

In this instance, the reason for the moment was not welcome, but this outcome most certainly was, especially for me.

It's a moment of love that I witnessed.

And it was the moment my dad decided to recover.

Getting to Know the Doctors

My mom and dad were opposites when it came to any medical issues.

My dad had none. I don't get it. He never dieted; he didn't exercise (until he was forced to at age 94). His belly grew as he got older, which is motivation for me to minimize that for myself.

He might have had issues, but he never expressed them. Once when I was visiting them in Florida, I woke up and heard my father whispering to my mom. I asked him what was wrong. He said nothing was wrong, but then said he thought he should go to the hospital. I asked why. He said he had a pain in his leg. I said, why don't you take an Advil. He said "What's that?"

Imagine being 90 and asking what an Advil is! At that time, I called Advil "candy," since I took so many of them while playing tennis.

Dad got a lot colder as he got older. He lost a lot of hearing. Other than that, he had no illnesses. He took medication for blood pressure and cholesterol.

When he broke his hip, they okayed his surgery because he was deemed strong enough to handle it. One day when I went to see him in rehab, he was very loopy from the narcotic. The last thing I wanted was for him to lose his mind. I told the staff not to give him the narcotic. I can only imagine the pain he had to endure, but I wanted to preserve his mind. The next day when I visited, I asked how he was and he said, better than yesterday. So I felt this was the right thing to do.

He was instructed to do lots of physical therapy, which he did. Whatever they told him, he did. No more, but he did what they said.

According to my dad's surgeon, 90% of people who break their hip in their 90s die within a year of the break. My dad lasted five more years. He always had to use a walker, but he was mobile and functional.

My mom was a different story.

As she got older, she started to focus on every ache and every pain. It started gradually but it became all-consuming the last few years. Even an eyelash stuck in her eye was a big issue.

Ultimately, Mom wanted to take a pill and wake up feeling completely healed. I mean, who wouldn't want that? But it's not going to happen.

I had the names of my mom's primary doctor, eye doctor, neurologist, internist, rheumatologist, gastroenterologist, vascular doctor, and proctologist. I had conversations with most of these doctors. My brother did as well.

I lost count of how many times I went to the local CVS (in Los Angeles) or the local Walgreens (in Delray Beach, Florida) to pick up an over-the-counter or prescription drug for Mom. The OTCs included Pepto-Bismol, Phillips Milk of Magnesia, magnesium citrate, Nyquil, Preparation H, hemorrhoid suppositories, Kaopectate, Pepcid, Senna Plus Laxative plus Stool Softener, Gas X, Dulcolax, Lidocaine, and Salonpas patches. These were scattered all over the house, many of them with expired expiration dates. I frequently had to Google the shape and number of a pill to find out what it was.

This doesn't include the variety of topical ointments, many of them with CBD, which admittedly, I took back home with me when I cleaned up the apartment.

Medicines requiring a prescription included meloxicam, quetiapine fumarate, acetaminophen methocarbamol, lorazepam, tramadol, prescription Zantac, and gabapentin. Some of these had disastrous results and were discontinued immediately (including the quetiapine fumarate).

Then there was the hydrocodone.

When Mom first started going to doctors more frequently, she was still independent. She made her own appointments (which she never stopped doing), got to her own appointments, and had relationships with the doctors.

I wasn't involved. My brother wasn't involved.

It was while my folks were living with my brother in LA at the height of the pandemic and my mom's constipation was going through one of those extremely rough periods, that my brother made the connection between the hydrocodone and the constipation.

Much to her angst, we weaned her off that drug and, for a period, her stomach did get better.

But, upon reflection, I realize my mom went to so many different doctors and they didn't communicate with each other, despite the fact they were all part of the same network and could read the info provided. They each prescribed my mom pills. She was overmedicated at times. The pharmacies/pharmacists didn't say anything either.

What better way to shut up a complaining old woman, who wants to be without pain, than to give her a pill? It's the easiest option.

When both my brother and I got involved, these doctors suddenly were more cognizant of what they would give her. Yes, this infuriated my mom in that she didn't have control. But the doctors were now looking at what she was getting and treating my mom more like they would treat their own mom (I have to say it helped that when my brother talked to each doctor the fact he was a lawyer somehow got into each conversation. True, he's an entertainment lawyer, but if you have experience negotiating with actors, directors, and studios, you can handle anything).

Mom had legitimate issues including loss of eyesight from macular degeneration, sciatica, stenosis, and especially the ongoing issues with her digestion. The digestion issue never had a definite reason for it. Some impressions from different types of scans included cricopharyngeal bar with an associated Zenker's diverticulum. This is a common symptom of chronic gastroesophageal reflux. But it was inconclusive if this was the crux of mom's issues (she had digestive issues much of her adult life, but more manageable when she was younger).

The reality is that we are all responsible for our own care. When I was in my 30s and broke my leg, I had to negotiate an extension of my physical therapy between the insurance companies and doctors.

At some point we all need help with this.

What is the right time to step in and help your parents despite its not being what they want?

There is no easy answer to this.

Maybe they will recognize they need the help and ask.

Maybe not.

Either way, I do think it's key to keep them part of the conversation and actively participate in their care.

In hindsight, what I wish I had articulated more effectively to my mom: It takes a team to give your parent the best care. The team's center is the parent. The support around the center includes doctors, pharmacists, home aides, and family. We all want the best for you.

The Financial Realities

I'm sure it's not a surprise to anyone reading this, but our health care system is broken in this country. It has been for decades. I'm aware of it as a solo entrepreneur and having to deal with high premiums with high deductibles.

Even more tragic is how much money you need when you age.

If you need 24-hour care 7 days a week to stay in your own home, $1 million will last about 4 years (as of this writing). One million of your hard-earned dollars will be used to have someone bathe you, feed you, and wipe your ass.

What do people do who don't have this kind of money and don't qualify for Medicaid?

There are some pooled trusts (such as the Theresa pool trust in New York, which might expand to other states), VA benefits, and long-term care insurance that could help, but when you need more help, most likely these will not suffice.

Plus, if you have some sort of pension, you may not qualify for some benefits. My dad's pension was too high for him to get some VA benefits.

My mom had long-term care insurance. My dad didn't because they didn't look at options until he was 80, and companies won't give policies to people over 80.

Luckily, they looked before prices skyrocketed. They managed to find a policy that had no end date although there is a maximum they will allow per day and per month.

Initially, my mom mainly needed the assistance for food shopping. There was someone coming in two days a week for 4-5 hours a day. That increased to three days a week, but nothing on the weekends; my mom was thrilled about that.

Everything was fine—at first.

But when it became apparent that they needed more help, and they were resistant to more help, it got more tense for my brother and me.

After much negotiation/arguing/whatever you want to call it, I got my mom to agree to more help during the day (4-to-5 days a week, with a few more hours each day). This took a lot of persistence.

I also knew that what Mom agreed to wouldn't be enough at some point.

The first hurdle was when Dad broke his hip. After rehab he needed around the clock care—this would be out of pocket. Through a social worker at the rehab center, I found an agency that was less money. We were also able to put some of the hours on my mom's policy.

The 24-hour care lasted two weeks. My parents dropped the evening help after that, so it was 16 hours. Gradually they dropped it to 8 or 12 hours. They decided it was enough extra help, and they did have my mom's aide a few times a week.

All told this started in July and ended around Thanksgiving. After that they were headed to their winter home in Florida. The out-of-pocket cost for in-home care for four months was about $20,000.

This was my first realization of how much in-home care would cost in the future.

My parents were lucky in that the aide who came for my mom also helped my dad. He was easier, but still agencies usually charge more for a couple. The agency we were with needed to charge more, but they agreed to only $10 more an hour, which was significantly less than other agencies. (We told Dad it was only $2 more an hour. Yes, we lied!)

After my dad died and my mom was on her own, with her

limited sight due to her macular degeneration and her slowly worsening dementia, the need for her to get more help was critical.

She agreed to five days a week, but not on the weekends or in the evenings, and she agreed to more hours (about 8 hours a day).

So, we paid a little more, but it wasn't financially significant.

Timewise, for both my brother and me, it was significant. I spoke to my mom from San Francisco every evening and Andy (who lived in LA) went to her house for one day of the weekend. On the other day of the weekend, I was on the phone, sometimes five to ten times a day, making sure she had her breakfast, and hoping that she might be willing to go downstairs to see people and get another meal. Sometimes there were leftovers and sometimes I ordered her food for the evening.

In March 2022, Andy was scheduled to be in Europe for a month. This would mean my mom would be alone for several weekends. This wasn't acceptable. I told her she needed to get help one day on the weekend because I would not be coming down to Los Angeles every weekend. Fortunately, her two aides agreed to alternate Sundays and my mom agreed.

After my brother came back, one of the aides continued to come some Sundays.

The need for help 7 days a week became more urgent. Another aide was sent on a Saturday, but my mom fought it and sent her away.

It wasn't until my mom got scared, a combination of Dad being gone and the dementia slowly progressing, that she stopped fighting and more help arrived. The last few months of her life she had 24-hour care.

No one has a crystal ball, and no one knows when one is going to die.

I did a financial analysis in Excel, and it was apparent that we would run out of money in 4-5 years if my mom stayed home.

She refused to move and I'm not sure how we would have moved her.

She did consider downsizing and moving to a studio, but the savings in rent would be a drop in the ocean.

My analysis showed at $30/hour for around-the-clock, in-home care 7 days a week, the money would last 4.75 years. If she were to move to an assisted living facility, it would last about 10 years. This was for a higher end assisted living facility (around $11,000 a month in 2022). A lesser one could last even longer. But moving into assisted living would mean great stress for Mom who'd be moving into a place with lots of people she had no interest in meeting.

I do regret bringing up the financial realities to my mom. I don't think it expedited her desire not to live, but I know it caused her some stress when she thought about it.

She left before a significant amount of money was spent on in-home care.

In many ways we were lucky.

THIS FINANCIAL REALITY HAS TAUGHT ME A FEW THINGS:

- As your parents age, encourage them to move into a community that offers the continuum of care (from independent living to higher end assisted living and memory care) before they need it, so they have time to get used to the different types of care. My dad would have moved into one years before, but my mom thought of it as death. In fact, my mom would rather die than move into an assisted living facility. So, she did.
- For my friends close to my age, look at communities where you can live for a long time on your own and then have

- available other options for when you need a different type of care.
- While you can't control when you will die, if you, your parents, or your partners have a pension, it's better to die earlier in the month so the beneficiaries get more money!
- While my dad didn't realize all the financial realities for when he and my mom would become more dependent, he did set them up with his financial advisor, so that my parents would live a comfortable life when they were older.

This was smart and fortuitous.

After dealing with these financial realities, I'm trying to grasp my own financial realities and my options. I struggle to find the balance between living now and saving for later.

I'm coming to an understanding that I oscillate between living the next twenty years in financial fear of the last years of my life and making smart financial decisions now in order to be prepared for those last years.

While my perspective changes frequently on this, I've decided to live with acknowledging the financial realities of aging while enjoying my life now.

What calms me down is when I remember Dad's quote: It'll work out. And if it doesn't work out, it worked out.

Stumbles and Falls

Dad, around 96 or 97.

Prior to my dad breaking his hip at age 94, he fell.

A lot.

Falls that could have ended his life there and then. We all witnessed one fall where he smacked his head against a tree.

Hard.

He got right up.

But Mom was concerned. A cousin was concerned. Andy was concerned. I was concerned.

My dad wasn't.

At least he wouldn't admit he was concerned.

He wouldn't admit he fell.

He told the doctor he stumbled. He wouldn't recognize a cane or walker could help him.

Yet he was very hesitant at times when he was out and about. He was much more relaxed when he would get to the supermarket or any large department store. He would grab a wagon, straighten up, and walk with more determination.

How an intelligent man doesn't recognize that the wagon was like a walker shows that stubbornness can easily exceed intelligence.

About six weeks before my dad broke his hip, I was visiting my folks in Florida, and I was on an errand with my dad. He finally admitted that he knew he should use a cane, but he didn't want to.

After he broke his hip, he used a walker. We skipped the cane phase or it was short lived because even Dad knew the walker was safer.

Dad still fell after he broke his hip mainly due to being lightheaded or off balance. Those falls didn't involve him going to the hospital, but the paramedics had to come once or twice to check him out and to see that he was coherent and fine.

His last fall was his last day. He wasn't feeling well and when he got up, presumably to use the bathroom, he fell and hit his head. He never regained consciousness and died that evening. Not a horrible way to go.

For most of the final years one thing I did not worry about was my mom's balance. She was very mobile, without the use of a cane. I wasn't concerned that she wasn't using one. When she did start to use one, it was her decision. No one told her to use one.

There were a few incidents where she fell but unrelated to her balance. It was more related to the unevenness of the floor, or if carpet stopped and there was a very slight difference in level to the hardwood floor.

In 2017 she took too much medicine one night to go to sleep. My dad got up in the middle of the night to use the bathroom and on his way his walker ran into my mom snoring heavily on the floor. He called 911 and they took her to the hospital. She blamed my dad, but he did the right thing by calling 911. When she berated him on day two of being in the hospital (she was released that day) I came to his defense and said how would you feel if you got up in the middle of the night and bumped into him. It must be scary.

The other time was after Dad died and I took Mom to Florida. I gave her half of a 5mg Ambien because she wasn't sleeping. I woke up in the middle of the night to a thud. Mom was on the floor. She was conscious. She denied she fell and had no memory of it in the morning. Needless to say, I did not give her any more Ambien, much to her chagrin and attempts to lure me into giving it to her.

Her final fall was when she broke her hip. She died two days later.

Both my parents died soon after a fall. Besides dying in your sleep, it seems to me an easier way to die than many other possible ways.

My dad had many stumbles and falls before the final fall. My mom had very few.

This leads me to believe that, while being smart about protecting your balance and doing all sorts of workouts and exercises in your 40s, 50s, and beyond to maintain it, ultimately something will happen.

Dad was stubborn and wouldn't use any assistance until he fell and broke his hip.

Mom voluntarily used a cane and ended up falling and breaking her hip.

Dad was fortunate that he had a quality of life for the five years after his broken hip. Most people don't.

Life is full of stumbles and falls. Whether or not that's your final action, it's what you do in between the stumbles and falls that matters.

Managing the Aides

My mom had a long-term care policy that was rare in that there was no expiration date. Most of the policies have a two- or three-year expiration—meaning, when you start using the services you have a certain number of years *in total hours* that it can be used. So, if it was a three-year policy, it could last twice as long depending on how long it took to accumulate the hours.

Around 2013, my mom started using her policy maybe once or twice a week. My parents oversaw it all—getting a home care agency, contacting them, facilitating what the aides were to do, etc. My mom changed aides often for various reasons. Reflecting on this, we were lucky that there was an abundance of aides, because in various parts of the country there is a shortage.

Initially they were there to help my mom shop and cook. It's important to know that for long term care insurance to kick in, the home care agency has to list at least two of the six activities of daily living where their services were needed. The six standard ADLs (activities of daily living) are: bathing, dressing, toileting, transferring (getting in and out of bed or chair), eating, and continence.

The longer time went on, the more my mom needed the aides. Of course, she resisted. To get her from two days during the week, to three days, then to four days during the week, required an act of Congress! She absolutely refused to have help come in on the weekends.

For a while this worked. Then for a while this didn't work, but still went on like this.

After my dad passed, my brother and I arranged for help to come in on the weekends. While mom initially resisted, she eventually gave in when it was the same aides she had during the week who alternated on the weekends. This was a good step forward and transition for when she would need around-the-clock care.

As the number of times aides came to the house, the amount of time I spent coordinating their schedule increased.

It takes a special kind of person to work with the elderly. I couldn't do it. It requires a patience that I know I lack.

With that being said, no one cares more about their clients/patients, than the people who love them the most.

Some aides are wonderful, some are awful. One agency sent an aide who was almost as old as my mom (supposedly a good cook, but still, how would this work?) When my mom told me about this woman, we both had a good laugh as we recalled the movie "Murder by Death," which was a spoof on all the detective movies. At the beginning of the movie, a woman is wheeling another woman into the room. Everyone assumes the woman in the wheelchair was Miss Jane Marple. Turns out the woman pushing the wheelchair was Jane Marple. The woman in the chair was her nurse! My mom was heading into that situation. This aide didn't last long.

Some aides worked for a while, quite a while, and when they took things personally that my mom said to them, they got upset and left.

Sometimes my mom was happy they left, other times she was upset herself.

At the end we were working with two agencies. The original agency started to send unqualified helpers and that proved to be stressful for my brother, as he was the local contact and had to sometimes go over to our Mom's to get involved.

We found a new agency, higher price, but the help for the most part was very thorough. The reason we kept the older agency is there were two aides who had been with my mom for several years. It would have been devastating for Mom (and those aides) if we ended with that agency and those two helpers with whom she had a relationship stopped coming.

During the last few months of Mom's life, the aides were there 24 hours a day. I used a spreadsheet to keep track of who was going in to help my mom and it changed every week. In addition to people from both agencies, we had my niece's former nanny's sister and her other sister (got that?!), who we paid out of pocket.

The agencies and the aides were on my speed dial.

When there was a crisis—an aide was late, a new aide came and my mom felt uncomfortable with them, etc. -- I was on the phone with the agency or with the aide, or both.

Many of my conversations during the week with my mom were about who was coming. I would remind her every day who would be there next.

So even though someone has full-time help, someone still needs to manage it. If that person is a family member, that tells the agency and aides that you're on it and watching.

I created the list below before my mom had full time help. This is what the aides were asked to do from 1—7PM (she wanted them out before "Jeopardy!" started).

Regular Tasks

First thing: When you first arrive, see what my mom has eaten, and if she took her blood pressure pill.

ON A DAILY BASIS:

- Clean her bathroom, especially around the toilet areas.
- Make sure there isn't excess dirt under my mom's fingernails.
- Make sure Mom's bed and nightstand are organized.
- Kitchen and dining area should be clean at the end of the day.
- Throw garbage out daily. Garbage chute at the other end of the hall, storage bins in basement.
- Make sure dinner (leftover food and plates) are all put away prior to leaving.
- Run the dishwasher before leaving. If there isn't time to put the dishes away, they can be put away the next day.
- Whoever is there on Friday, make sure there is food for the weekend. (Go over the food with my mom.)
- Make sure my mom knows where things are in the refrigerator.
- Make sure my mom wears the panic lifeline button when you leave.
- Make sure the television is set to either "Jeopardy!" or the TCM channel.
- Make sure the door is locked when you leave.

AS NEEDED:

- Laundry
- Please throw out expired or bad food in the refrigerator
- Sweep floor
- Clean counter
- Make sure there is enough Ensure, Gatorade, bananas, cheese, crackers

Many times items above were overlooked. There was always expired food in the refrigerator and it's hard to organize a nightstand if my mother didn't want you doing it.

Funeral Arrangements

My parents made their own funeral arrangements many years before they passed. I knew about the arrangements, but I didn't realize what a blessing that would be for me.

They planned the arrangements when they lived full time in Florida. They used a local chapter in Delray Beach that was part of the Dignity network, which was a series of chapels across the country. They also purchased Away From Home insurance to cover travel and transportation costs. The reason they did this was they were spending more time in California and they were to be buried in New York. They needed to have a local chapel coordinate travel of their remains to New York and have most of the costs covered.

This turned out to be very serendipitous.

I was stuck at San Francisco airport for over three hours when I was flying down the day my dad was dying. When I needed the flight to be on time, it wasn't only late, but extremely late. Not knowing what to do and realizing my dad was most likely not going to make it, I pulled up the information I had for the funeral insurance.

I made one phone call to the *Away From Home* insurance and gave them my dad's insurance number. They provided me with a local contact number in Los Angeles. They explained that the local contact would, when the time came, pick up my dad, and dress and ship his body.

The time came late that night.

I called in the morning. The mortuary immediately got Dad from the hospital where he died. Since it was a Sunday, they said they would have more information on Monday morning and someone would call me between 9:00 and 9:15. They called as promised.

I found everyone involved to have very high customer service skills and standards. There were a few additional costs, mostly due to the adjustment in airfare. But it wasn't much.

I couldn't imagine, with the grief and stress of the moment, what I would have done if I had had to start making arrangements at that time, not to mention how costly it would have been. It was hectic enough with everything else I needed to do; how I could have handled even more stress?

Earlier in the year that Dad died, he was wondering if it would be financially better to be buried in Los Angeles.

I did some research—my parents' plot was bought with the New City Jewish Center in New York—buying a group plan cost less to purchase. However, it doesn't have any resale value.

In Los Angeles, and especially since they wanted a Jewish location, it was at least $15,000 for each plot.

I told my dad this and told him it wasn't worth it. For that money, we could fly business class, stay in nice hotels, and see some shows.

Upon hearing this, he said to stay with what we had in Westchester, New York. He'd be buried near friends. But he asked me not to see a Broadway show the night of his funeral!

When my mom passed, the process was even easier. Since it was fresh in my mind (Mom died less than 18 months after my dad) and I had updated my notes, I could bypass initial steps and contact the Los Angeles local chapel directly.

I urge everyone reading this to make sure their parents have made arrangements.

2020.

The Pandemic

I feel I handled most aspects of the Covid-19 pandemic in a very calm, logical, rational, and sensible way.

I didn't panic about most things.

The pandemic shut down travel and it was the first time I was home for an extended time without traveling for work. I loved it! Fear and shock were there, but I also realized that people were going to an extreme. If you could get the virus from touching food items from the grocery store, a lot more people would have gotten Covid than they did. Therefore I didn't even think of wiping down my groceries when I got home.

I was able to discern what made sense to do and what not to do.

While I never lived through a pandemic before, I had lived through an epidemic. I came out as a gay man in my late 20s when AIDS was rampant. If I had sex the wrong way, I could die. Literally. I had to learn quickly how to have a good time, live my life, and not die.

I applied those thoughts to how I dealt with the pandemic. I figured out that I could go on walks and hikes with people. I walked a lot on my own. My mask was lowered but if I came upon someone, I would cover my nose and mouth. Tennis was everything! As soon as we could, many of us got back on the courts and played several times a week.

Many of my friends judged me and thought I was being irresponsible. It's interesting to note that every single one of those friends got Covid before I did. Enough gloating!

Instead of panicking whether my business would fall apart, I looked at other possible options I could venture into if my current situations did fall apart. Interestingly and fortunately, both my bookkeeping and teaching businesses flourished. I intentionally started teaching less since my bookkeeping business grew. I am forever in admiration of my fellow business owners.

I achieved a sense of calm, control, and acceptance around a world event that I had no control over, which felt good.

Except for one thing. Well, two things.

Mom and Dad.

Early in 2020 I had flown to Los Angeles to take my parents back to Florida. This was the trip where I realized my mom had what I diagnosed as mild cognitive impairment. But all in all, they could take care of themselves. They had help during the week and had friends and some family around them. So, I felt fine leaving them, knowing I'd return in a month to pay a visit, and then come back in March to take them home to Los Angeles.

I went to Florida in February 2020 and the trip went without any incident.

We all know what happened in March 2020.

The thought of my parents' being across the country without knowing what the future would bring stressed me out to no end. One of my friends, who I know is all doom and gloom, said to me: where do you want your parents to die? (meaning in Florida or in California.)

Of course, I wanted them to come back to California but my father refused. In early March the cases were up in New York and California, but Florida was pretty low. I knew it was just a matter of time before the cases grew in Florida, but no amount of logic could persuade my dad. My mom wanted to come back to California, but my father refused. He told me if he was wrong, he had had a good life, that it was okay.

This was one decision I couldn't accept. I lost sleep, and woke up in mid-March with a fever of 101. Naturally I thought I had the virus, especially since I had been traveling for work the week before.

I did not have the virus, and I realized I had no choice but to accept my father's decision to stay 3,000 miles away. So I spoke to them several times a day and went about my life, adapting to the circumstances of our world.

My brother did not accept my father's decision.

He kept persisting with my dad, trying to convince him that the best decision was for them to come back to California. Where I had stopped, my brother persisted.

An unrelated incident happened that changed my father's mind. A friend of theirs died, not from the virus, but of other circumstances. My dad realized that, if he were to get sick, he would want to be around family, so he relented and said they would come back to California.

My brother decided the best way to keep them safe was to take them back to his house and have no one see them except him.

I didn't like this idea, and in hindsight that is an understatement.

In theory my brother's idea was correct. Logistically, it was destined to fail.

While my parents didn't have around-the-clock help at this point, they did have help five days a week. I couldn't figure out how my brother could maintain his full-time job and also take care of both of them. I was concerned about the many raised steps in my brother's house, as they presented a risk. My parents ended up falling multiple times while they were at my brother's house.

It was only a matter of time before my life would change due to a decision I didn't make.

Andy on the right, me on the left.

Sibling Rivalry

When Jessie, my youngest niece, was about 10 or 11, she had a birthday event where everyone played laser tag. If you're not familiar with laser tag, it's a live action game, like paintball. Unlike paintball, nothing hits you, rather your gun gets deactivated for a few moments. Somehow, they keep track of points, so I imagine if you play a lot, you can develop a strategy.

At this party there were two rounds of play.

In the first round, everyone, kids, and adults alike, played. In the second round, all the kids played and only two adults continued—my brother and I.

When I asked an adult later why they didn't continue playing, she said she had an issue shooting at children. Apparently, most of the adults felt this way. I was taken aback by this. That's not how I thought about it.

I just thought there weren't many activities where kids and adults can go all in together and have a great time. I had so much fun and all the kids who I interacted with did as well—a couple of kids purposely targeted me, and it was fun.

I bring this up because, as mentioned, all but two adults had an opposite opinion on this.

My brother and I shared the same values here.

Those shared values bound us on many different levels, values that I believe we got from our parents and kept us close.

Despite this, we had our rivalries when it came to taking care of our parents.

Lots of them.

This makes sense since dealing with aging parents is a very stressful situation without a happy ending.

Any issues between siblings that had existed but were never resolved simmer below the surface. These issues will explode when stressed. Dealing with elderly parents caused that stress, and boom, it all exploded.

Now, I love my brother and he loves me. We know we can trust each other implicitly. We share a common journey.

But we also push each other's buttons. I found him to be opinionated, judgmental, and abrasive at times.

He would say the same thing about me.

These opinions of each other boiled over during the pandemic.

At one point we threw more four-letter words at each other than what was said in any Quentin Tarantino movie. More than an episode of Succession. More than the New Jersey mob in the Sopranos.

You get the point.

My mom could sense tension between my brother and me during May 2020, when they were living with my brother, and I was in LA for the month. I talked to her a little about it.

When we got back to their place, I heard my mom tell my dad that both of us (my brother and I) were not talking to each other. When my dad heard that he made a comment, something like, "I might as well just die as opposed to them fighting over me."

This prompted me immediately to go up to him and say "don't you dare. He'll blame me for that as well!"

I could come up with a laundry list of the reasons I was angry at my brother.

But I'd rather remember the laser tag story.

Why?

It's the antithesis of sibling rivalry. It's the innate bond we share from our upbringing. We have so much in common. Yet stress led to a lot of infighting, not talking for a period, and regular conflict.

When both parents are gone, the stress, worry, and conflict are gone.

Or they should be.

I know someone who speaks to no one (his dad or siblings) after his mom died.

Another friend lost her relationship with her sister-in-law after her brother died.

I have two cousins who are brothers who never spoke again after their mom (my aunt) died.

The tension between my brother and me is G-rated compared to all that.

I do know that any sibling relationship, whether it was close or not, will change once what tied you together is gone. I know my brother and I had a relationship prior to the years of taking care of our folks, but honestly, I can't remember what that was like.

But if your relationship was strong before, it will prevail. I can't speak to the opposite because that wasn't my experience.

Maybe it's harder when you have a good relationship and dealing with this. If you didn't really get along with any of your siblings, you may not really care about their opinion or what they are thinking.

What I do know is its okay to go through this experience getting bruised. It's not permanent.

Mom and me after Dad passed—
but he's framed on the couch!!

Dementia and Stubbornness

The last five years of her life Mom went from mild cognitive impairment to early-stage dementia. For most of her life, she was stubborn.

It sometimes was difficult to distinguish between the two. Being stubborn was a survival skill for Mom, a method of independence.

The dementia scared her. She once asked me, when referring to the dementia, how will I know what's real or what's imaginary? I didn't know how to answer that question.

Her way of dealing with that uncertainty was to increase her stubbornness.

This made Mom very defensive at times. Her doctors, sometimes her aides, were idiots. The F word got used frequently.

Being scared resulted in her calling 911 a few times or thinking about calling 911. One time she called me first and I told her not to call 911 because she needed an enema.

Mom got frightened a lot. She asked me what should she do if she became frightened? I told her to call out to the aide, who was in the other room.

It was her fear that ultimately led us to have around the clock care for Mom.

I have no idea how I would react if I couldn't see well and had the beginnings of dementia. I most likely would get scared as well.

Mom focused a lot on her ailments. If it wasn't her stomach, it could the spasms in her leg, eczema on her face, or arthritis in her finger.

About one month before she died her desire to live decreased dramatically. She said to me "Why am I here? I mean on this earth?"

Personally, I got scared when her stubbornness lessened. While I think that sometimes it kept her from making decisions that would have been beneficial for her, the stubbornness was her fuel. It was her way. She wasn't going to change.

In my last conversation with her, when she was in the ambulance heading home from the hospital after she broke her hip, she was slurring her words (which she was cognizant she was doing). Despite that, she said to the EMT several times, can you give me some privacy?

Mom valued privacy and stood up for it until the end. She was stubborn to the end!

Hospice

When my brother suggested we get Mom on hospice, I felt it came out of left field—I had never thought about it. But he had heard from a friend of his that hospice is not just for the last few weeks of your life. If there's a qualifying condition (such as dementia), you can get hospice care.

When I looked at the website for the agency that was recommended to my brother, I did see dementia listed. But my mom's dementia was early stage. So, I was dubious that we would get hospice and wasn't sure how the initial meeting would go with hospice and my mom. I figured they wouldn't take her on.

What I forgot is hospice is a business, and the bigger the hospice company, the more people they will take on. My brother said the initial meeting wasn't even to examine my mom. In the initial meeting they already considered her part of hospice—the meeting was to get her in the system.

We used Vistas Healthcare, which is a very large hospice agency. I had heard that Vistas never takes anyone off hospice. I was certain my mother would be one of the longest lasting patients that they had or would ever have!

The benefits of hospice are plentiful. They provide medications and medical supplies at no cost. For my mom they also provided a person to come to her house to do massage, and a chaplain available if she wanted someone to talk to.

Hospice did not take the place of having to hire home care aides, which we now had to do 24/7. Any hospice nurse who came to see my mom was in addition to the home care aides.

Hospice, as most people know, is care and comfort to keep someone out of pain. They aren't helping one improve but are there so you can live as comfortably and fully as you can.

My mom had had stomach issues for a long time. Constipation was regular for her, the juxtaposition of those words intended. When it got bad, she said it was like trying to get the rock of Gibraltar through the eye of a needle. That sounds painful.

But then, she would be better for a bit.

At first, I wasn't in favor of hospice because I thought she'd be on it and then she be let go from it and we would've gotten used to some of the services. But my brother witnessed first-hand the everyday pain in person more than I did, and most importantly my mother was in favor of it.

I became hopeful when hospice said that my mom should be as active as she could be and they encouraged that. I hoped that the support of believing she should be more active would rally her.

The downside of hospice, particularly when the hospice company is large, is it's difficult to navigate through their system. I can't tell you how many times in one day I had to call hospice to find out when people were coming to my mom's place and why they didn't show up—there was no centralized coordination. There was some expensive medical equipment at the house that I tried to have them pick up after Mom died, but they never came over. That is one example of how disorganized the organization was.

My mom fell and broke her hip in the early morning of December 26, 2022 (the Federal holiday). A word of advice: Do not let your loved ones have an accident on Christmas! Half of hospice was out that day and that intensified the un-organization of the agency.

Hospice sent her to the emergency room, where she stayed most of the day. This was puzzling, to say the least, since hospice isn't about their clients having surgery. Most likely they sent her to the emergency room since they were short staffed and there wasn't anyone from hospice who could stay all day with her. This is very disturbing, although if they hadn't sent my mom to the emergency room, I may not have realized the severity of the situation and may not have gotten down to Los Angeles as soon as I did.

After she died, we needed the death certificate from the doctor in the agency. This is required for my mom's body to be able to get on a plane. With my dad, it was easy, the hospital sent it over. In my mom's case, it took them almost 24 hours to get it over. Once they did, the initial report had the secondary cause of death as falling and breaking her hip. The woman at the mortuary told me this would trigger an investigation from the LA police or social services department to make sure my mom wasn't abused.

This would delay the trip back East and that would mean the funeral would have to be delayed. We had to get on the phone several times and get the doctor to take the secondary cause of death off the death certificate. This apparently does happen quite a bit. (I was lucky to have it go smoothly with my dad.)

Ultimately, Vistas did their job. Even so, I would recommend if time permits, looking at different hospice agencies. Not having experienced it ourselves, perhaps a smaller hospice organization might be better organized and more focused on each patient.

God Forbid and God Willing

My dad's financial advisor would often say when talking about my parents, God forbid something happens to them. He would use this expression quite a bit.

My brother used it once and I challenged him on that.

Especially the five years before they passed, death was pretty much around the corner. I mean it was more inevitable for them than for me, my peers, and my nieces unless some tragedy prevailed.

The expression God forbid didn't make any sense to me. I knew that God's will would be more benevolent when death came than God's forbidding.

I did not want my parents to die. There was a time where I thought they were invincible, as many of their peers passed away and they were still standing and active.

Whether it was a combination of selfishness and desire for my parents to live with quality and not just to live, I could never say God forbid to the prospect of their dying.

I knew when that moment happened it would take me by surprise, and indeed it did both times.

Either way, I'm glad I never used the term God forbid because I think that's the denial of the inevitable final journey that we all eventually take.

I Saw my Mom Die

I'm not sure the memory of this will ever fade. It's a moment, a moment that will forever be embedded in me. It's the hardest moment of my life up till now.

Reflecting on this, what would life be like if you knew all along you would see your mom die? What would it be like for my mom to know that her eldest son would be there when she died? These are questions that really don't matter. It's the life before that moment that matters. Nonetheless, it's something I've contemplated many times since she died.

I was determined that the week of Christmas would be as normal for me as possible. I was staying home for the first time in a few years. I had a few parties back on after the pandemic and I was going to have some downtime.

I had a plan for the beginning of the year. I was heading to LA. I was going to work with one of Mom's agencies. We were going to take away her access to her pills and administer them to her so we had more control over when/if she was medicating. We were also going to monitor her diet. Our hope was that she would gain some strength, which might give her some desire to be more active which could create a renewed purpose to live.

I had told her of the plan to give her some hope that her pain could be lessened.

The weekend of Christmas went without incident and how I wanted it to go and continue through the week. I did speak with Mom Christmas evening—she sounded low, which is how she had been sounding for some time. So, it wasn't anything unusual. That day my brother was in New York, and I was home in San Francisco.

We both got a text in the middle of the night saying Mom had fallen and was in a lot of pain. They were recommending morphine. My brother and I spoke, and we agreed that a low dosage of morphine could be given. Up until now we weren't allowing morphine. We had morphine in the house, given to us by hospice, but only one caregiver and I knew where it was.

Eight hours later I found out Mom broke her hip, and I knew I had to get to Los Angeles.

This fall took place early morning December 26, which was the Federal Christmas Day holiday that particular year. As already said, this meant that half of the hospice staff was off. This was also the year that Southwest canceled most of their flights due to a software problem. All flights, buses, and trains were booked. It took me several hours to secure a car rental, which was not an easy thing to do since everyone wanted one (I didn't want to drive my car or a friend's car because I wanted to fly back; I only wanted to drive one way).

By the time I got the car rental, it was night and a severe rainstorm had just started. I waited until morning to drive down.

The evening before I drove, I got a call from an ambulance driver who put my mother on the phone. She hadn't realized she had been in the hospital most of the day. I told her I was coming down the next day and she asked me if she had known that. I told her, no, she hadn't known, but I was coming down because she had broken her hip. She asked if she was going to have surgery, and I told her not at this time.

This was the last time I ever spoke to her.

When I got to her place the next afternoon, she was asleep and breathing very heavily. I didn't realize she was in a nonresponsive state and that type of breathing was her body shutting down. No one told me this. Maybe I was naïve or purposely ignorant, but I thought she was resting, finally resting after the ordeal, having gotten 5 low doses of morphine within 5 hours. I realize this sounds ridiculous upon reflection, but

I had no experience with any of this. The doctor didn't tell me what was happening when I spoke to him. He did say she had only weeks to live (only when I asked him), and the next 24-to-72 hours would be telling, but he didn't tell me she could DIE in the next 24-to-72 hours. This is one of the biggest gripes I have—I wish they had been more direct with me. Why couldn't he have just said she could die in the next three days? I would have heard that.

Would that have made a difference? Yes.

By hearing she had weeks I decided that I would stay in Los Angeles for the duration and I would stay at her apartment. For most of that year, I had been staying at my brother's house because I found being at my mother's was much to handle. But it wasn't that way now. If I needed more stuff, I'd have a friend send it down. I can work anywhere so I can work in the apartment. It was a matter of weeks.

If I had known that my mom could die in the next couple of days, I would have moved Alexa immediately into the bedroom and played the music that Mom loved. I planned to do that the following day.

Despite not having slept the last two nights, I would have stayed in her room. I'm eternally grateful for our caregiver (Betty) for coming to me and telling me to get in the room right away because she realized something was about to happen. I got to Mom as she took her last breath. I was in a state of disbelief and remember I said "Ma, no" as she died.

My brother didn't think he would be back from the East Coast in time to see her, but I told him he had plenty of time since he was coming back the next day. I wouldn't have said that to him if I thought it could happen any time.

At first, I felt very guilty about all this. One of the books I read about grief differentiated between feeling guilty and feeling sorry. This helped me a lot.

I'm sorry I didn't put on the music and stay in the room.

I don't feel guilty.

She died about 1:30 in the morning. Around 7:30 the night before I heard a noise from her room. Both the aide (Anita) and I ran into the room. Mom was awake, being vocal, but completely incoherent. I said "Mom, Mom, what is it?" and the aide said "Lila, Howard's here." She mumbled a few words and then went back into unconsciousness.

When the aide and I discussed this right after it happened, we both thought she had said "I know" in response to Anita's comment that Howard was here.

A couple of hours later when I was going to try and get some sleep, I said good night to my mom and told her I loved her. I told her I didn't know what I would do without her.

But as I was leaving the room, I thought that's not a great last thing to say to her, I don't want her fighting to stay alive if it's her time to go.

So, I then said, *don't worry Mom, I'll be okay, I'll figure it out.*

There must've been a part of me that knew she would die otherwise I wouldn't have said that to her. It did seem like a natural thing to say after finding out she only had weeks to live.

I wish I had been able to have one more conversation with her when I got to LA. It's one thing to say you want to die when it's theoretical; it's another when something happened and that choice, if you have a choice, is in that moment.

I wanted to talk to her and ask her what she thought about having surgery for the broken hip if she qualified to have it. I would have mentioned the extreme pain she would endure and how the strong pain pills wouldn't help the dementia.

I would hope she would have decided it wasn't worth it. But she never had the chance to make that decision. Funny enough, the one time I wanted my mom to have the last word and she doesn't get it.

Instead, I had to make that decision for her, essentially by keeping things as they were. I paved the way for life to end for the person who gave birth to me.

I doubt she would have qualified to have the surgery. (There is an irony that my dad, who was not athletic for most of his life, qualified to have surgery to fix his broken hip at age 94, but my mom, at age 92, who played sports her whole life, wouldn't have qualified. My dad survived 5 years after the surgery, my mom passed less than two days after she broke her hip.)

This still gnaws at me. My brother says I did a mitzvah (a Hebrew word for a good deed), this would have been her decision, what she wanted. I do believe that's true, I do believe it was the right decision.

But it doesn't make it any easier.

Epilogue

Someone I know was surprised at my grief. After all, isn't it natural for parents to go first? Am I not grateful for someone my age to have had my parents for so long? There must've been something about the dynamics with my parents to cause such grief.

This guy is a doctor. You think he would have had a bit more understanding and compassion.

The guy who cuts my hair lost his parents when he was in his 30s and felt it must be harder to lose them when you're older because you're so used to having them around.

Seems a bit wiser than the doctor, doesn't it?

But the doctor got two things correct:

- I'm extraordinarily grateful for the gift of my parents for over 60 years of my life. Despite the stress of the last 15 years, the blessings outweighed the burdens.
- And yes, our dynamics were special.

TO MY DAD:

You showed me you can teach an old dog new tricks. I feel like our relationship deepened after you were 80. Of course, it's also my growing up that allowed this to happen, but it takes two. No one will ever show interest in what I do the way that you did. You were thrilled to listen to how my business was going, and how I built my business, just because I was your son. You expressed pride with both your sons going for things in business that you never pursued. You expressed gratitude that both of us were able to keep our businesses going through the pandemic.

Dad, you were an anomaly! You have no sense of diet or exercise, and yet lived to 99 with your mind intact. You showed me, if I have to choose, and it's not a great choice, which is more important, the body or the mind? It's the mind. With the mind you still have a sense of purpose in this world. You still have a sense of nostalgia, regret, appreciation, and basic human emotions that we all take for granted for most of our lives. Because of this, not only do I keep in physical shape, but I actively do mental exercises to keep my mind stimulated.

I used to think it would be better if you went before Mom.

I was wrong! Well, at least for me I was wrong, I know that's what you wanted. You told me once that if Mom went first you wouldn't last more than a week without her.

Against all odds, you not only survived five years after breaking your hip. You also survived a bout with pneumonia. Nonetheless you adjusted and had a sense of relevance and purpose until the end.

One day you were there, the next day you were gone.

I was in shock. I was sure you would live to 100. I feel you left before completing a sentence. I was looking forward to more even though you had already been there in abundance.

TO MY MOM:

You were the opposite of Dad. You externalized every ache and pain. An athlete your whole life, you used that competitiveness to try and rally against what was thrown at you. From sciatica to stenosis, macular degeneration to early-stage dementia, all overshadowed by the major digestive issues you had, it was an uphill battle and you had enough, as you told me months before you died.

There were many times I went to the supermarket, opened the freezer door, and then closed it to look inside. It was all blurry and I know that's how you saw all the time once you got macular degeneration, because that's how you described it.

Even knowing that, I admit my irritation and annoyance could overshadow my empathy.

Your demand to be noticed and not ignored is something you had your whole life. I believe this served you well and also made things more difficult for you.

As you got more dependent on others, specifically me, that demand could get exhausting, so at times I felt like whatever I did wasn't enough. In hindsight, I think all I wanted was for you to feel better. I was thrilled on those rare conversations when you didn't complain about any pain. I was glad when, at age 90 or 91, despite the pain, you wanted to hit a tennis ball. Yes, we were both on the same side of the tennis court, and Andy spotted you, but you did hit the ball a couple of times. Those brief moments brought you some feelings of accomplishment.

I had to learn not to let my outlook be affected by your outlook, while trying to feel empathetic. I'm not sure how well I did.

There is no one who drove me crazy more than you. There is no one I miss more than you.

TO BOTH MY PARENTS:

To reiterate the quote that Dad said to Andy: *it'll work out. And if it doesn't work out, it worked out.*

As I've gone and still go through my grief and disbelief you both are gone, I am being guided by Dad's wisdom. While he didn't live his life that way, the fact that he came to that conclusion and told my brother, who told me, is a gift for the two of us.

It is my hope that I take the best of both of you to serve me the rest of my life. Your absence leaves a hole in me that will never be filled, and I don't think it's supposed to be. When I think of the rest of this year, and next year, and the year after that, and you really, really aren't here, my insides collapse a bit and the ground drops beneath me.

How lucky I was to have you both vibrant and independent for so long.

Even bad memories are good memories.

And for that, and for everything else you both were for me, I am.

I don't miss the burdens. I'm still recovering from the burdens.

But what I wouldn't give for one more blessing.

What I Learned Along the Way

- If someone is unresponsive and breathing abnormally and heavily, they are shutting down and will die sooner than later.
- Self-care is vital. Be more forgiving of yourself.
- You are stressing yourself out more than helping them when you start arguing with them.
- Understand the finances. If you don't have those skills, find someone you trust who does.
- Dementia can qualify you for hospice.
- Research hospice agencies before you need one.
- I used to think if you had to pick one, mind or body, you'd pick the body. Now I'd pick the mind.
- Understand the differences between long term care, hospice care, and home agency care.
- When you say you are getting old, you're not actually old yet.
- I thought it would be "better" if Dad went before Mom, which is what happened. But I was wrong. (Although that's what Dad would have wanted.)
- Morphine is used under hospice when the end is in the near future.
- Get your parents to make funeral arrangements.
- Be team centered. The doctors, pharmacists, and health care agencies should talk with each other. You will need to coordinate this. And keep your parents involved.
- Enjoy the quiet boring moments with them. They are special.

Things I'm Grateful for During This Time

- The user of humor and levity
- Keep good documentation of everything related to them
- Trying to pick the battles worth fighting and letting go of the others
- That my parents made funeral arrangements
- That I did financial analysis on costs for various options in taking care of my parents

About the Author

Howard Miller is the owner of Fulcrum Point Partners, which provides bookkeeping services to business owners. Howard also facilitates team building and brainstorming sessions, provides coaching to entrepreneurs, and teaches management skills.

"Burdens & Blessings, A Lighter-Hearted Approach for Middle-Aged Folks Dealing with Aging Parents" is his first personal book and third book overall.

An avid tennis player, poker enthusiast, and semi-coordinated country dancer, Howard got his competitiveness, independent spirit, and twisted sense of humor (as much as they would deny it!) from his parents.

Howard grew up in the Bronx and Rockland County, New York, and received his bachelor's degree in Math and Computer Science from the State University of New York at Albany. He has lived in San Francisco for the last several decades.

You can reach him at howard@fulcrumpointpartners.com.

www.ingramcontent.com/pod-product-compliance
Lightning Source LLC
Chambersburg PA
CBHW060205050426
42446CB00013B/2993